ANDERSON JONES

MAIN CHARACTER

Anderson Jones, affectionately known as The Dude, didn't set out to be an author. However, his love of space, learning and sharing his knowledge just naturally led to telling stories on paper. He has been known to tell elaborate stories about what can happen in a black hole and how meteors fly through space. When his mommy saw how fascinated he was with her book, she asked him if he wanted to write a book about space. After an enthusiastic yes, she walked him through the process and he enjoyed every minute of it. Now, he's an author…with many more books to come! When Anderson is not obsessing over planets, volcanoes and Roblox, he likes to play with legos, play-doh and his cat, Onyx. If you ask him what he wants to be when he grows up, he will quickly say astronaut. The Dude reaches beyond the stars…because he wants to see what's outside of the Milky Way!

Anderson had always been curious. He wanted to know how things worked, like "Where does the water go after you take a bath?" "How do the lights work?" "Where do apples come from?" But more than anything, Anderson wanted to know how to get to space! He wants to be an astronaut and tells anyone who will listen all about the planets. He's always looking for someone to talk to about how cool outer space is and here you are! He's going to be so excited to see you! Ready for an adventure? Let's go!

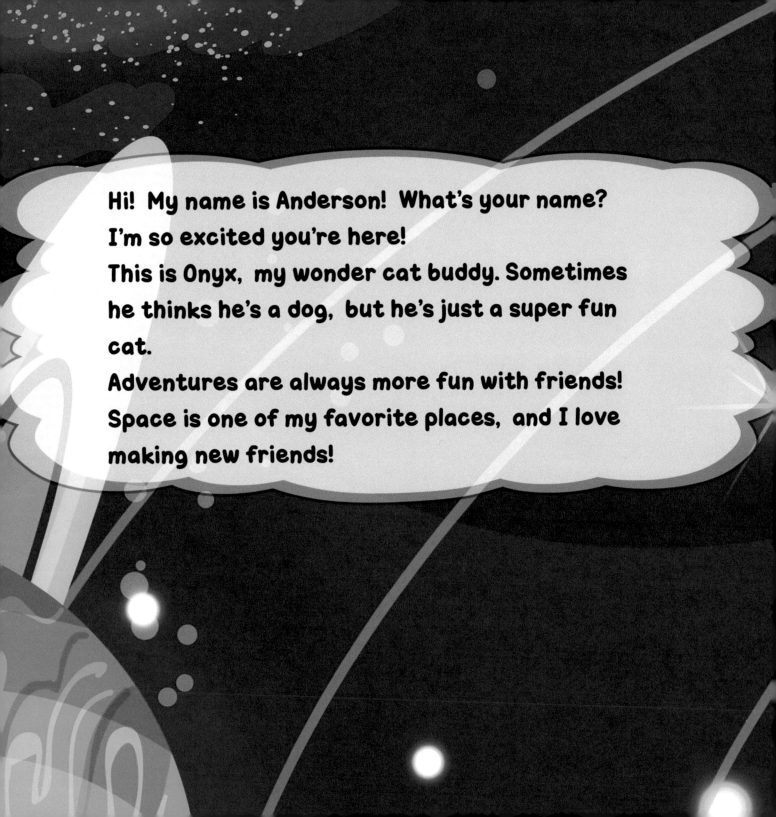

Hi! My name is Anderson! What's your name?
I'm so excited you're here!
This is Onyx, my wonder cat buddy. Sometimes
he thinks he's a dog, but he's just a super fun
cat.
Adventures are always more fun with friends!
Space is one of my favorite places, and I love
making new friends!

We made it! Do you like our spacesuits? Hope so, because they're SO expensive! Today, if you build one from scratch, it would cost around $250 million! Sounds crazy, but spacesuits aren't clothes... they're tiny, human-formed spacecrafts! These suits have to protect us from the sun's radiation, vacuums in space, and things zooming through space that could poke holes in regular clothes. Spacesuits also have to provide oxygen so the astronauts can breathe! If you're having trouble hearing me, turn up your headphones. Space is SUPER quiet! Sound can't travel here, it's like bedtime here... all the time... dark and quiet. But don't close your eyes.We have planets to see!

SUN

That's the sun, it's our galaxies closest star. Yes, the Sun is a star! We can't stay long because it's WAY too hot! The Sun's surface is 10,000 degrees! The Sun was born 4.6 billion years ago! That's way WAY more than Grammie's mommy and Grandpa's dada! The Sun is 93 million miles away from Earth. You'd have to say, "Are we there yet?" a bazillion times! The Sun is also SUPER big, like gigantic! You could stuff one million Earth's into the Sun.

MERCURY

This is Mercury! It's the smallest planet in our solar system. It doesn't have any moons and no cool rings. But guess what? If we lived on Mercury, we would all be older! One year on Mercury is only 88 days, so your birthday would come way faster! My favorite thing about Mercury.. the side that faces the Sun is super hot and the other side is super cold!

Here we are on Venus! Lots of people call Venus the sister of Earth because they're almost the same size. Venus is the hottest planet... way too hot to play outside... so maybe we don't want to live there. At nighttime, Venus is the 2nd brightest object in the sky... after the moon of course. My favorite thing about Venus... it spins the opposite way of Earth AND has more volcanoes than any other planet! The floor is probably always lava!

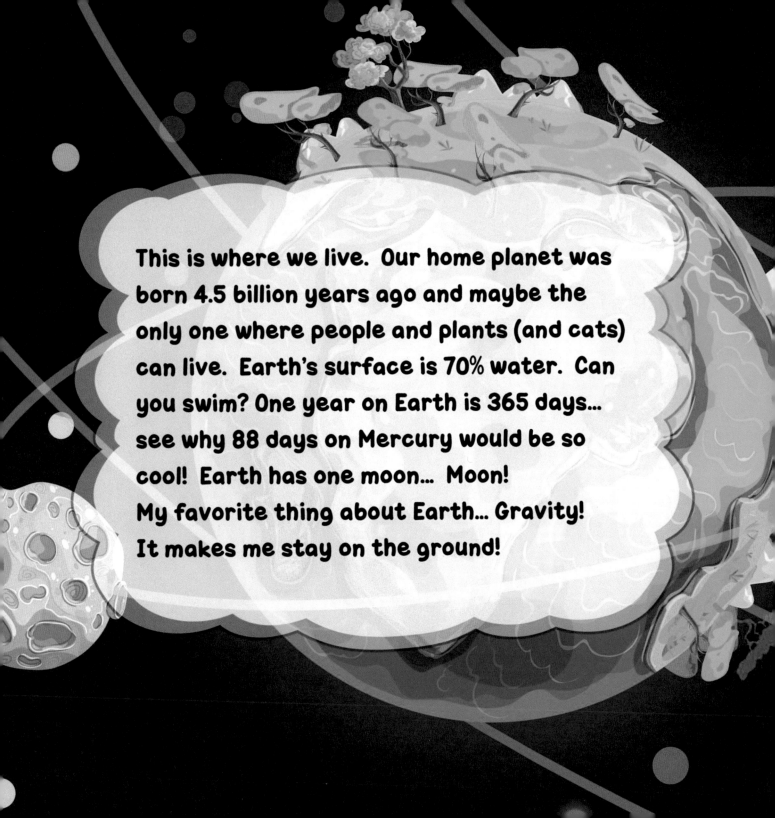

This is where we live. Our home planet was born 4.5 billion years ago and maybe the only one where people and plants (and cats) can live. Earth's surface is 70% water. Can you swim? One year on Earth is 365 days... see why 88 days on Mercury would be so cool! Earth has one moon... Moon!
My favorite thing about Earth... Gravity!
It makes me stay on the ground!

MARS

Mars! A long time ago people nicknamed Mars the Red planet. Know what? Mars has the tallest mountain in the solar system, Olympus Mons. Scientists think it might still be an active volcano! Pieces of Mars have been found on Earth, that's so cool! The sky during the day on Mars is kind of red and sunsets are blue! My favorite thing about Mars... the super big volcano!

Jupiter is the biggest planet in our solar system. If you put all the planets together, Jupiter is still 2 and half times bigger! One day on Jupiter is 9 hours and 55 minutes... the day can really get away from you! There is a huge storm on Jupiter that has been going for 350 years! My favorite thing about Jupiter... it's the biggest!

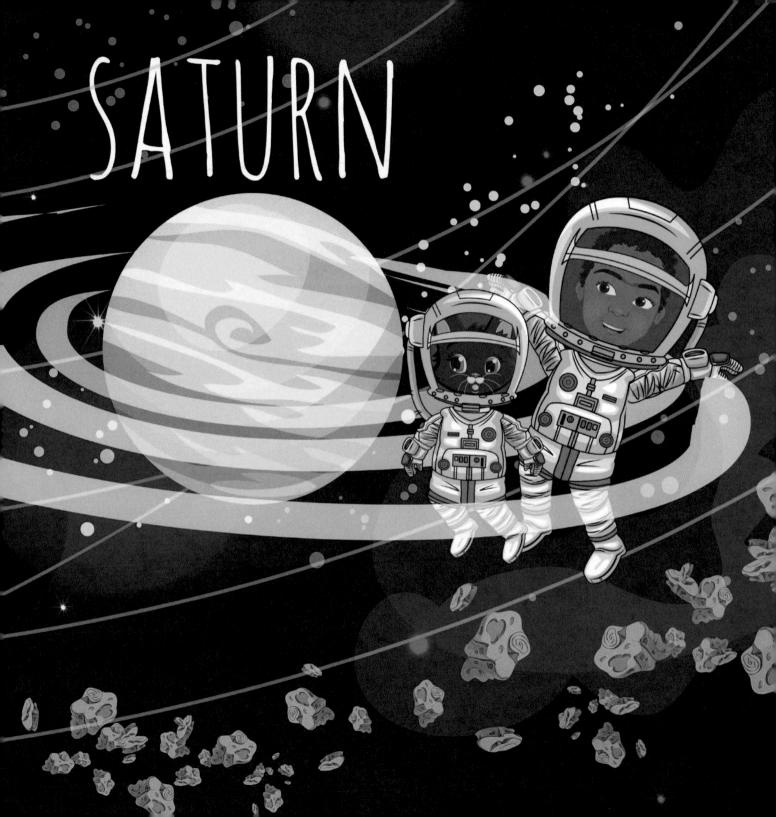

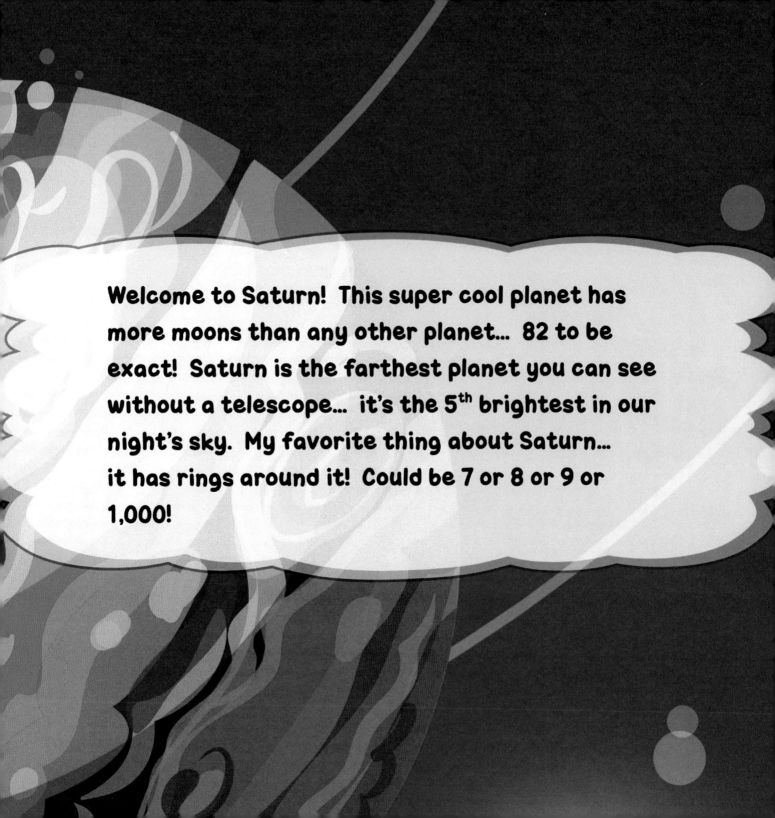

Welcome to Saturn! This super cool planet has more moons than any other planet... 82 to be exact! Saturn is the farthest planet you can see without a telescope... it's the 5th brightest in our night's sky. My favorite thing about Saturn... it has rings around it! Could be 7 or 8 or 9 or 1,000!

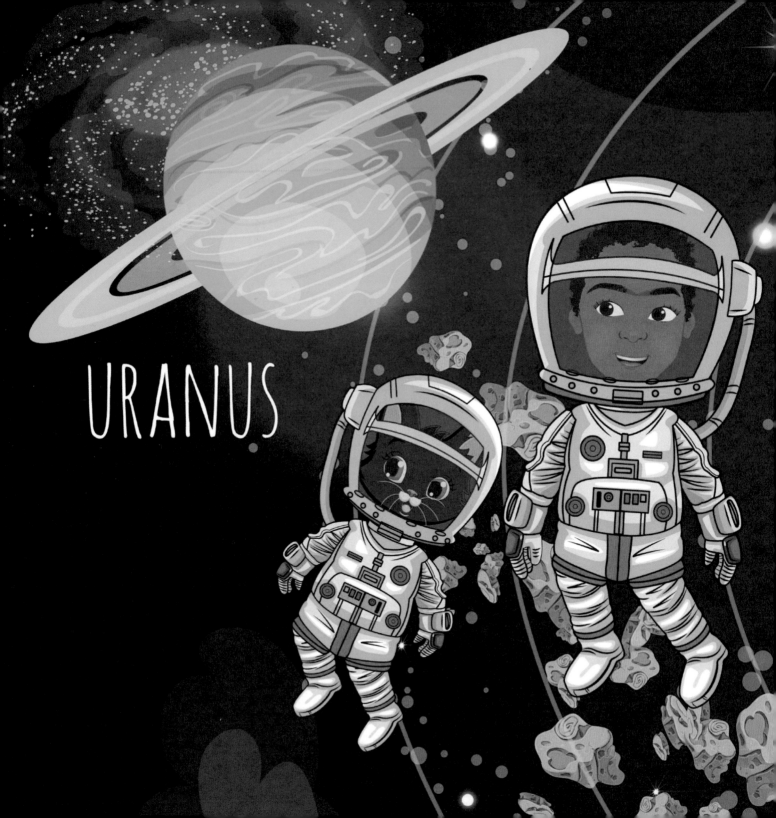

URANUS

Uranus is super, duper cold... the coldest! You can't dress warm enough to be there... so let's not stay too long! The planet's surface is full of ice crystals, which makes it look light blue. It takes Uranus 84 Earth years to go around the Sun. Uranus has rings too! Not as many as Saturn, but it's still cool. My favorite thing about Uranus... it's funny because it spins on it's side like it's sleeping!

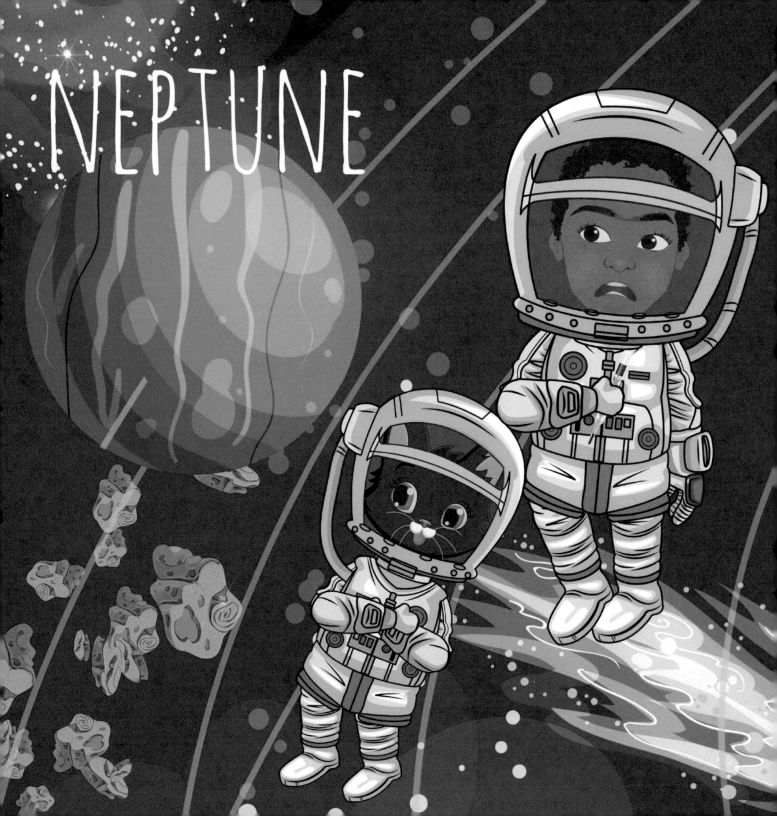

Neptune is the eighth planet from the sun... it's SO far away. One year on Neptune is equal to 165 years on Earth! Neptune has 14 moons and really big windstorms... they are SO fast... way faster than our tornadoes! My favorite thing about Neptune... it's SO far away and the coldest... ICE COLD!

That was so much fun! What was your favorite planet in our galaxy? Did you know there are lots more stars and planets out there? Outer space can go forever and ever! And we didn't even talk about the drawf planets, black holes, comets... there's just so much out there! What do you want to be when you grow up? There's so much to explore!

See you next time!

COPYRIGHT

Anderson Takes On Space

A Children Story Book

Contact: Jones.thaisa@gmail.com

Written by: Anderson Jones & Thaisa Jones

Illustrations by: Hermain Fatima